INFINITE STARS

by
Gayle Bong

American Quilter's Society
P. O. Box 3290 • Paducah, KY 42002-3290

Acknowledgments

This book has been an enjoyable and satisfying challenge thanks to my friends. My sincere thanks is extended to Gayle Bielanski and Pat Titus for their support and encouragement in this project, and to Tracy Lancour for her encouragement and review of portions of the manuscript. Thanks also to Sue Bong, Pat Titus and Gayle Bielanski who have been very eager and willing to help me perfect these techniques as they made their quilts. I am also grateful to Linda Bohling and Rose Lauchart for their help in finishing my quilts. Everyone's help was greatly appreciated.

Thanks also to Crosley-Griffith Publishing Company for granting permisson for use of "Cajun Spice" and "Spanish Moss" from *Judy Martin's Ultimate Book of Quilt Block Patterns*.

Photography by Bruce Thompson.

Additional copies of this book may be ordered from:

American Quilter's Society
P.O. Box 3290
Paducah, KY 42001

@$12.95. Add $1.00 for postage & handling.

Printed by IMAGE GRAPHICS, INC., Paducah, Kentucky

Dedication

To my daughter, Lisa, for sharing my enthusiasm
and being tolerant of my one-track mind.

Table Of Contents

Introduction

It wasn't as if there weren't any other quilts I wanted to make, but the 60° triangle ruler I purchased a while back had been sitting unused for too long. So equipped with equilateral triangle, grid paper, colored pencils and a pair of mirror tiles I began to draw. I always base my designs on traditional patchwork blocks and I proceeded to transfer a block into a diamond just as Jeffrey Gutcheon explains in his book, *Diamond Patchwork*. When I set the mirrors down on the points of the diamond, there was a feast for the eyes as a dazzling star shone back at me. Immediately, I saw that the possibilities were infinite.

After having been a template-free quilter for eight years, I didn't want to go back to templates. As much as I enjoy handling fabric, I could achieve better accuracy with rotary cutting methods. So, I applied the principle behind the template-free methods and developed the rules necessary to cut template-free 60° designs.

This book is not a basic quiltmaking course; rather it is intended to provide structure for the quilter who wishes to experiment with design and learn another aspect of template-free quilting.

In this book, I share the techniques I enjoy most in designing 60° stars as well as ideas for using the stars in the overall plan of the quilt. Border ideas are also presented, as these stars make great medallion quilts. I also review general rotary cutting and sewing tips for piecing you'll be proud of, followed by the template-free 60° method I use to cut the various shapes. Many of the techniques may be familiar to you; only the angle or math has been changed. I show the math involved so that you can see why and perhaps remember more easily how to cut each of the shapes. Templates are also included as well as suggestions for possible quilting designs.

I do not include patterns because that would be contradictory to the techniques presented in this book. The possibilities of unique stars are infinite. My goal in writing this book is to share the fun of designing quilts and to see new star designs at quilt shows and in magazines in the years ahead.

Chapter 1 ... *Designing a* **60°** *Star*

A point of a star is actually a part of a diamond. By changing the design within the diamond we can create an infinite variety of stars. The designs in the diamonds can very easily be acquired by converting a traditional patchwork block into a diamond. The traditional pattern may only be the basis of our new design as we explore some of the options in coloring.

Designing the stars for this book was an easy and enjoyable task. I can spend many happy hours drawing and coloring them. I suggest you approach designing a quilt like playing a game. Play the design game as long as you like. The more you play, the faster new ideas will come to mind and the better your designs will be. If you do not enjoy such a paper and pencil project, decide quickly on the design and proceed directly to fabric.

Supplies

The supplies you need to design a star include a source book of traditional patchwork patterns. A book such as Jinny Beyers' *The Quilter's Album of Blocks and Borders* would be great, as it includes a transparent grid overlay, which you may find useful in converting blocks.

You will also need equilateral triangle grid paper. This is a graph paper with a grid of triangles rather than squares. An equilateral triangle is one in which all three sides are the same length, all the angles are of the same degree (always 60°) and the perpendicular measurement to any side is always the same. You should be able to purchase this paper through your local quilt shop.

With our template-free methods, we will not need to draft our design to size or make templates. Instead, we will use our diagram on the equilateral triangle grid or graph paper to determine the measurements and the angles to cut the patches. I have included templates for those quilters who wish to use them.

You'll also need colored pencils to color the diamond in the various ways outlined here. To prevent you from having to draw the lines over and over, either photocopy the original line drawing or place tracing paper over the line drawing and color. To try different color combinations, use a new area of the tracing paper.

Another great tool in designing quilts is a pair of mirror tiles. If you draw one diamond and bring the tiles up to it, they will act like a kaleidoscope and reflect a six-pointed star. This will save you the time it takes to draw and color all six

diamonds when trying to develop a design you like. Look for mirror tiles at a hardware store or building supply store. They are usually sold in 6-packs of 12" tiles. Consider splitting a pack with your quilting friends.

Suppliers of the equilateral triangle, graph paper and mirror tiles are listed in the back of this book.

Converting Blocks Into Diamonds

As a quilter, you are probably familiar with the basic grid of squares upon which so many of our patchwork designs are based. Many quilt books show these designs with their underlying grids and have them categorized as to whether they are 4-patch, 9-patch, etc. blocks.

Equilateral triangle graph paper is used in a similar way as a basic grid. It is actually quite simple to convert a square block drawn on a square grid to a diamond using this paper. The first step in using the graph paper is to mark off a grid of diamonds with the same number of divisions as the block you are transferring. One of the first things you'll notice is that the diamonds on the graph paper are actually composed of two equilateral triangles. This will be very helpful in calculating sizes and in our template-free methods, but in transferring designs it can be confusing. Try to look at your grid as being composed of diamonds. After you work with the paper a while you'll become accustomed to it.

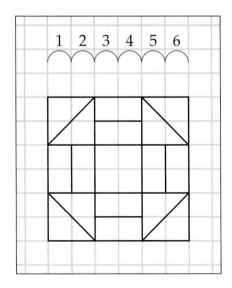

Fig. 1a: Square Block.

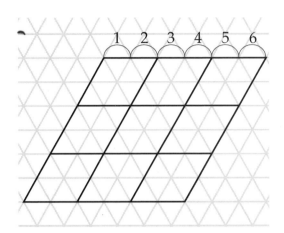

Fig. 1b: Diamond Grid Marked Off.

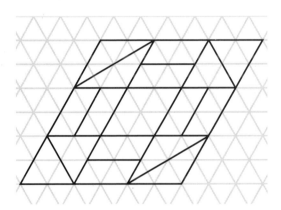

Fig. 1c: Block Converted.

Choosing Blocks

When choosing blocks to transfer, the rule to remember is: *The lines of the design must cross over graph lines where the graph lines intersect.* See Figure 2.

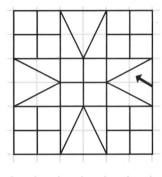

This line is not crossing the graph line where the graph lines intersect.

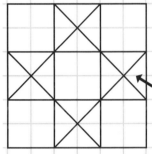

These lines are crossing the graph line where they intersect.

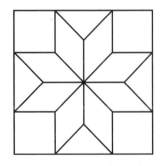

Eight-pointed Star designs are not based on a grid. This type of design shouldn't be chosen.

Fig. 2

Next, subdivide the diamond patches to correspond with the square patchwork block. Notice that a diamond can be divided in half diagonally either lengthwise or crosswise. This corresponds to a square divided diagonally. A diamond divided crosswise will result in two equilateral triangles. A diamond divided lengthwise will equal two half-diamonds. When dividing the diamond lengthwise, your line will be crossing the graph line between the two equilateral triangles forming the diamond. The Monkeywrench block shown above illustrates this.

You might find it helpful to have a line of the graph paper run parallel to the corresponding line of the block you are converting. Then transfer one row at a time.

Choosing blocks is a personal matter. You may have a favorite block you'll want to try or maybe you'll choose a block to symbolize something happening in your life. The blocks you choose need not be complex. You will see as you proceed through the book that delightful stars can be created using simple blocks.

Naturally, not all designs appeal to everyone. To find ⌐ that you will enjoy, transfer just the lines of several ┠· Then follow the coloring exercises explained next.

Coloring

After you have converted a numᵇ diamonds, make about eight photocoᵖ prefer, do your coloring over tracing paper. Color the diamonds in light, medium and dark tones. The placement of the colors is entirely your choice. You do not need to color the diamonds symmetrically, as the block was probably colored. You may even disregard the seam lines as you color it. Remember, you are only using the design or seam lines as a starting point in designing your star.

After you have colored the diamonds, use the pair of mirror tiles and set them down on the point of the diamond. When you look in the mirrors, watch for the shapes that form where the sides of the diamonds touch. You may want to recolor, reversing positions of the lights and darks to emphasize these shapes.

The Anvil pattern illustrates some of the choices in coloring a diamond. Use your mirrors to see how these might look as stars. For more options, turn your paper around and see how the opposite point looks as the center for the star. Occasionally you will find one that will sparkle when you use the opposite point.

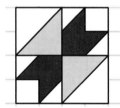 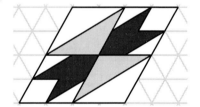

Fig. 3: Anvil Block Converted.

Fig. 4: Coloring Options.

It is important when using colored pencils that you don't merely change colors but that you also change the value of the color. Contrast is just as important to the success of your star as precision in cutting and piecing. It may be you don't like a star you colored because it lacks contrast.

If you have made some extra copies, you might want to find some children to do some coloring. You may be surprised at their perception of the diamonds. I keep my extra copies for when friends come over with their children. It keeps them occupied and they can enjoy coloring quilts for you because they know you enjoy them.

As you can see, there are many options in coloring the diamond. I would caution against too much coloring, though. Colored pencils just don't match the fabric. Nor is your coloring a contract that can't be broken. If you have any doubts about which color or fabric to use in a particular patch, cut a few pieces of different fabric and make a sample diamond or paste up.

Onto Infinity

Have you ever wondered where all the patchwork blocks came from? I imagine a good share of them were accidentally designed. Perhaps in drawing a block from memory or assembling the patches in the wrong order a new and pleasing pattern evolved. Remember, you are in control of the design and have the power to decide if a piece is in the wrong place.

When you think of all the different patchwork patterns and coloring options that can be used in the template-free 60° approach, it is no wonder that such variety can be created. By now, you have probably found the star you would like to piece. But, for even more fun and more variety why not try some of these designing tricks? Just add a line here or take away a design element there to expand the possibilities. Perhaps you can meet the guild challenge with your star.

Addition

I found Anvil patterns in two of my quilting books. Naturally, they were colored and obviously meant to be pieced in two different ways. Seeing the blocks colored in these two ways led me to coloring it differently. Then, I inadvertently colored my design by following the lines of the graph paper and not those of the block. I didn't see a need to correct that and soon I was changing and adding lines quite freely in other diamonds. In SPRING BEAUTY (pages 9, 10) I added to the big patch in the center diamond. In BLOOMING BEAUTY (pages 10, 11) I also followed the lines of the graph paper.

ANVIL STAR, 40" x 46".
Designed for use as a round table cover. A red table skirt will set off the star nicely. Uses coloring option in Fig. 4 (bottom row, left).

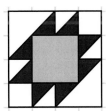 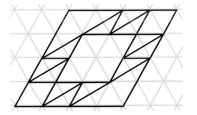

Fig. 5: Addition, Anvil Block.

SPRING BEAUTY, 36" x 40".

Fig. 6: BLOOMING BEAUTY Design.

Fig. 7: SPRING BEAUTY Design.

BLOOMING BEAUTY, 36" x 40".
These flower-like stars were based on another version of the Anvil block.

FEATHER TREE, 80" x 80", Sue Bong.
This Double Feathered Star began with the 5-patch tree block. The inner border was necessary to fill all the space.

Another example is in the FEATHER TREE quilt by Sue Bong. The original block was a 5-patch tree pattern. Remember our rule that the line of the design must cross over graph lines where the graph lines intersect? The lines of the tree trunk went against our rule. Rather than discard the tree pattern, Sue saw that there was a definite advantage to changing those few lines to meet our rule.

Look back at the blocks you converted. If there is a block that did not form a pleasing star, perhaps you can make some minor adjustments. If you add or change lines, keep in mind our rule that any new lines must intersect where the lines on the diamond grid intersect. You may also be altering the order of assembly.

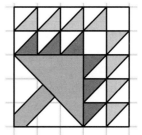

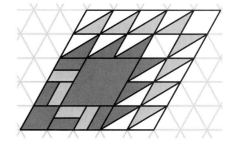

Fig. 8: Converted 5-Patch Tree Block.

Fig. 9: FEATHER TREE Design.

Subtraction

If you found it difficult to change or add a line or two, perhaps you'll find this trick a little easier. It's my favorite. When you set the mirrors down on the point of the diamond, did you include the complete diamond? Go ahead and move the mirrors. Trust me, you won't be arrested. Place them in a row on each side, keeping them on the graph lines. Almost like magic, a new design appears. Again working with the Anvil pattern, I designed the quilt PAINT SPLOTCHES.

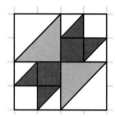 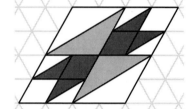

Fig. 10: Subtraction, Anvil Block.

Fig. 11: Design For PAINT SPLOTCHES, Based On A Revised Coloring Of The Block In Fig. 10.

The mirrors can be stopped along any row of the diamond grid. PINWHEEL PIE is the result of moving the mirrors in to include only the four patches in the corner of the Pinwheel Askew block. The resulting star is smaller, which enabled me to repeat it in a more traditional style quilt.

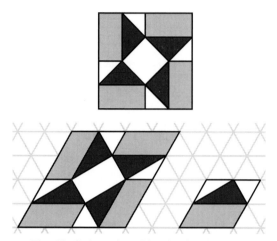

Fig. 12: Subtraction, Pinwheel Askew Block.

Fig. 13: PINWHEEL PIE design.

If you have converted any Pinwheel blocks into diamonds, you saw that the mirrors did not reflect them spinning in the same direction. To see them spinning in the same direction, it is necessary to draw out all the diamonds. The illustration shows how a pinwheel type diamond would appear in the mirrors and when six diamonds are drawn facing the same direction. You have the choice of piecing them as they reflect or as spinning in the same direction. If you piece them as they reflect, you will need to remember to cut half of the pieces in reverse.

Division

Another form of subtracting from the design, division, may be what your star needs. In this exercise, begin coloring the diamond. This time start coloring at one end of the diamond. Before you color to the other end, check the mirrors and see what has happened to the design. The portion of the diamond you didn't color will drop into the background and the areas you colored will be emphasized as the points of the star. You might want to study the reflection of the line-drawing before you color to decide which elements you want to emphasize or drop out.

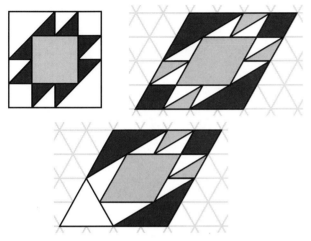

Fig. 14: Division, Anvil Block.

I used the Anvil pattern again with this trick. ANVIL V is the fifth in the series of quilts using the same block.

Fig. 15: ANVIL V Design.

Division has been used by quilters for some time. I think it is a little easier to practice when just coloring one diamond block. It is definitely something I want to try more of when I get back to making square blocks.

Multiplication

Yet another option for you to consider in designing your star is the way the diamonds are arranged, or your choice of sets. The 6-pointed star is the most basic star setting. Another possibility is a 12-pointed star. To reflect the 12-pointed star in the mirror, draw three diamonds together as illustrated.

Fig. 16: Anvil Block Used For Multiplication.

Fig. 17: Multiplication, Anvil Block.

Now, have fun coloring the diamonds, keeping in mind all of the creative options discussed earlier. The 12-pointed star is no more difficult to piece than the 6-pointed star. You'll just have to piece twelve more diamonds.

In the DOUBLE ANVIL STAR I treated the three diamonds as one big diamond and colored it to emphasize the shapes created where the blocks touched. There is no need to use the same fabric in the same positions in all 18 diamonds. In fact, it would probably make a more interesting star if you did change fabrics.

PINWHEEL PIE, 72" x 76".
Subtracting from the Pinwheel Askew block resulted in the stars in this quilt. Designed and pieced by Gayle Bong, quilted by Rose Lauchart.

ANVIL V, 42" x 42".
Designed and pieced by Gayle Bong, quilted by
Linda Bohling. The first attempt at leaving out
the points at the end of the block proved
successful.

PAINT SPLOTCHES, 65" x 85".
Subtracting from the Anvil block resulted in the
stars in this quilt, designed for a twin bed.

Fig. 18: Experiments with
Aunt Sukey's Choice
Block.

Fig. 19: Design for CAROL'S KALEIDOSCOPE.
Aunt Sukey's Choice plus subtraction, addition,
division and multiplication results in this unique star.

CAROL'S KALEIDOSCOPE, 74" x 80".
Aunt Sukey's Choice combines with all the designing techniques for lots of fun and a unique star.

DOUBLE ANVIL STAR, 65" x 66".

Varying the color in the outer circle of the Anvil diamonds resulted in a sparkling star.

Interesting Diamonds Based On Square Blocks

These diagrams show patchwork blocks, how they look transformed into diamonds, and suggestions for adding, subtracting, dividing or multiplying to create unique stars. Use your mirror tiles to see the stars. Remember that combining techniques and coloring options increases the possibilities. Use your tracing paper to color the diamonds.

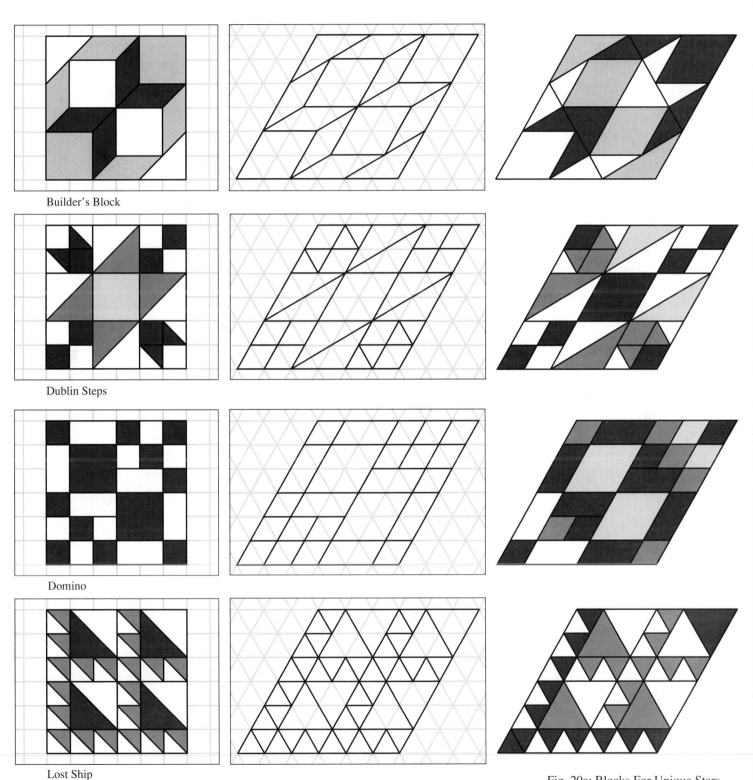

Builder's Block

Dublin Steps

Domino

Lost Ship

Fig. 20a: Blocks For Unique Stars.

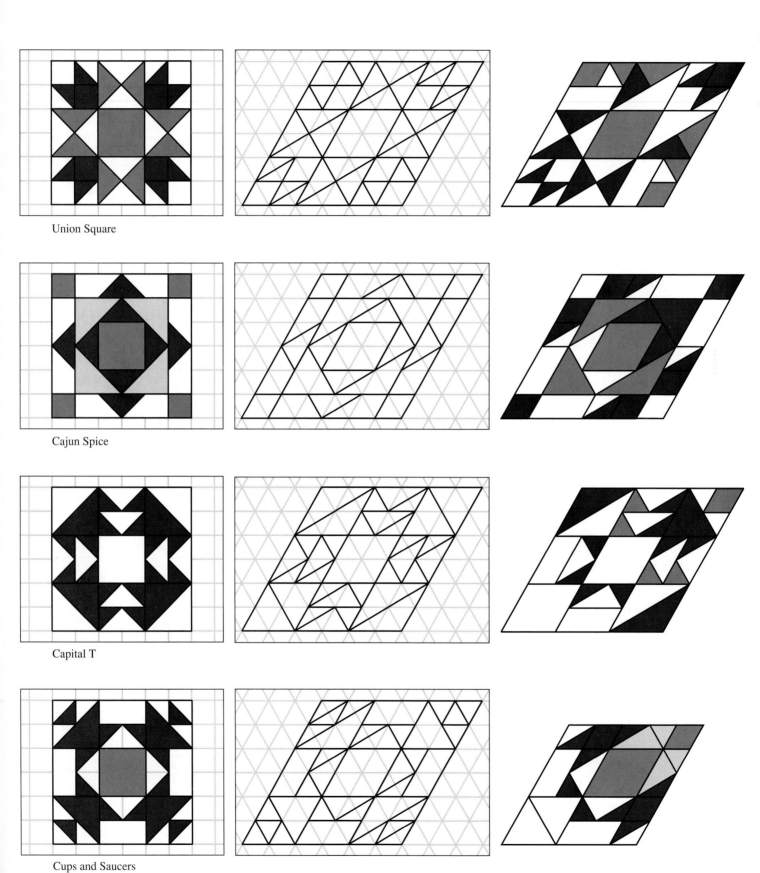

Union Square

Cajun Spice

Capital T

Cups and Saucers

Fig. 20b: Blocks For Unique Stars.

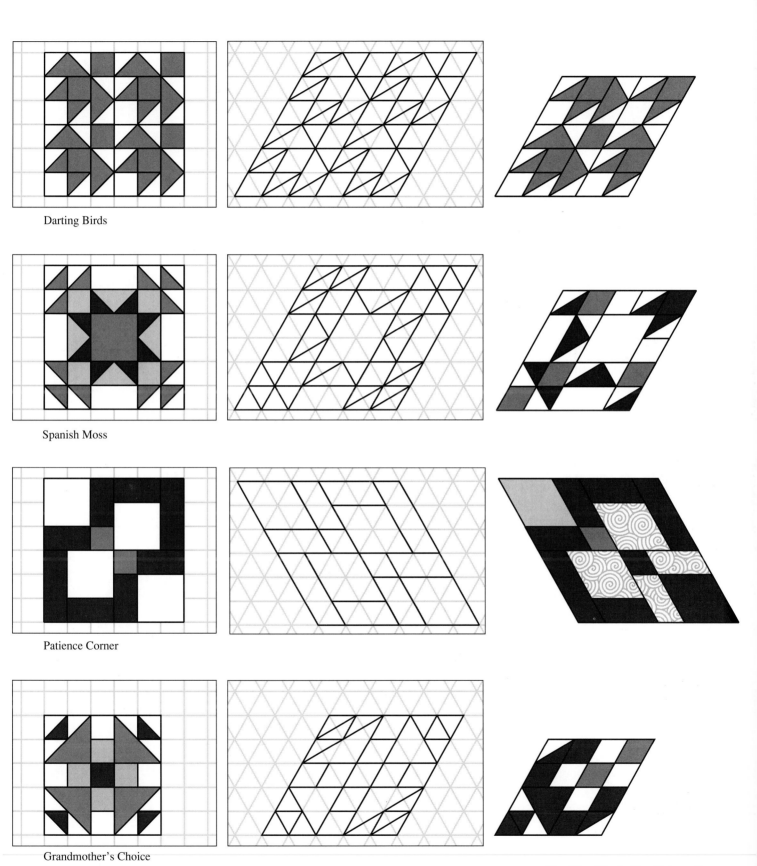

Darting Birds

Spanish Moss

Patience Corner

Grandmother's Choice

Fig. 20c: Blocks For Unique Stars.

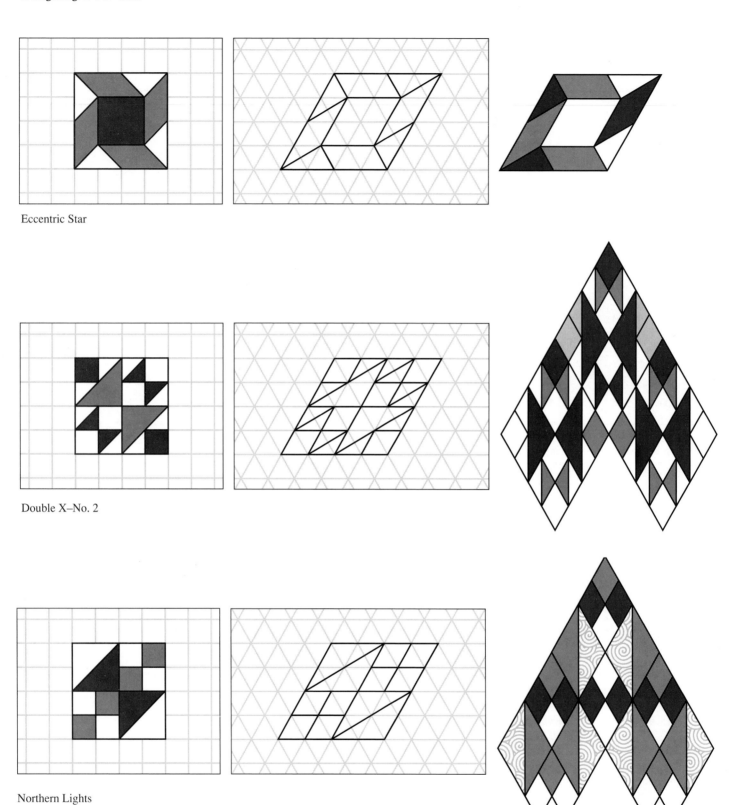

Eccentric Star

Double X–No. 2

Northern Lights

Fig. 20d: Blocks For Unique Stars.

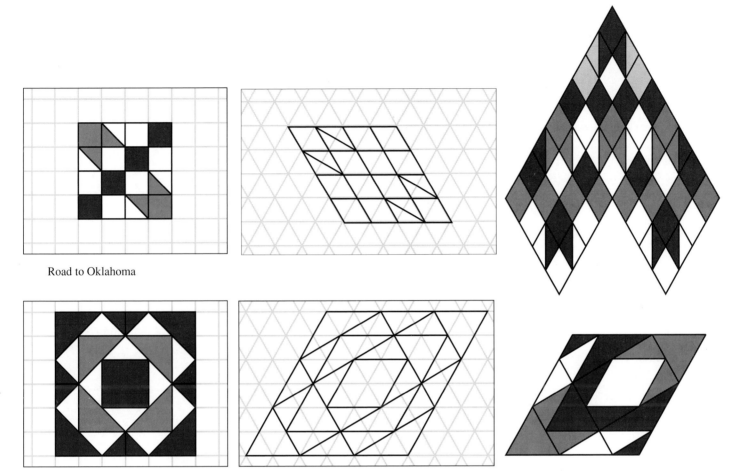

Road to Oklahoma

Gentleman's Fancy

Fig. 20e: Blocks For Unique Stars

Summary

I have suggested four ways to easily add creativity to your quilts. By adding or changing a line of the original block, or deleting part of the original block from either of the two ends, you will have a multitude of designs to color. These suggestions are a few of the possibilities for designing patchwork quilts. By experimenting, you'll find the same methods can be applied to traditional square blocks.

The arrangement of the patchwork blocks or diamonds has always been an option of the quilter. For more diamond block arrangements, I suggest you read Jeffrey Gutcheon's book *Diamond Patchwork*. He explores block piles and other possible configurations of the patchwork diamond.

Other techniques for designing quilts could also be applied to designing a star. You might like to try using more than one block in a 12-pointed star setting. Shading the blocks to create an optical illusion might be the choice of a quilter who wishes to experiment with color. The sky is the limit and we haven't even considered designs requiring templates. I hope you enjoy your journey and may you never see an end to an infinite variety of quilts, star or otherwise.

Chapter 2 ... *Designing the Quilt*

Once you have chosen the star, you will need to plan the rest of the quilt. Drawing the quilt on paper is recommended. It can help when determining yardage requirements and when assembling the quilt. Good plans will include background pieces and borders. And finally, the same diagram can be used when planning the quilting design.

The Shape

Quilts are usually made in two shapes: square or rectangular. A design based on the equilateral triangle will more easily form a rectangular shape. If a square quilt is desired, the background for the 6-pointed star needs to be cut larger and then trimmed square.

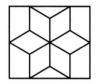

Fig. 21: Quilt Shapes.

A 6-pointed star would be good for a table cover or tree skirt, too, but these might best be finished in the shape of a hexagon. This is simply accomplished by the insertion of either six half-diamonds or full diamonds between the points of the star. They may be left plain or pieced. In BLUE FACETED DIAMOND, Pat Titus chose to set in pieced diamonds based on her original block to finish her wallhanging in a hexagon shape. This is actually another setting arrangement that could be squared off. (page 50)

The diagram of a 12-pointed star in figure 22 shows that this type of star can be finished as a hexagon, too. A drawing on

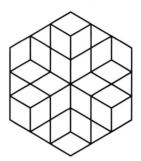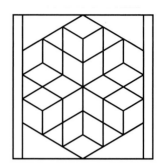

Fig. 22: Strips Added To Make A Square Quilt.

graph paper will indicate the size to cut the triangles and diamonds needed to fill in the background. Half-triangles are used to square the corners of the quilt. It may be left rectangular at this point or made square by the addition of two strips sewn to the long edges of the quilt.

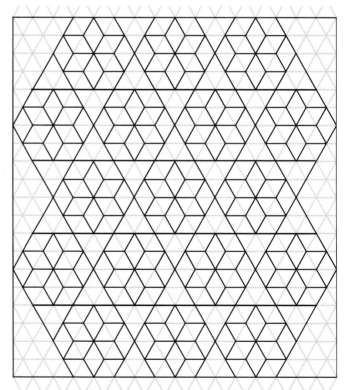

Fig. 23: A Rectangular Quilt Made From Diamond Blocks

Figure 23 shows the setting used for PINWHEEL PIE. The stars represent any small star, such as the pinwheel. For a setting like this the stars are first set into diamond-shaped blocks. The diamonds are then sewn into rows. With the quilt sketched on graph paper, the angles and sizes to cut all the background pieces are easy to determine following the formulas in the unit on cutting.

The Size

When making a quilt, I let the design guide the size of the quilt. The intended use of the quilt can also help in determining the size. To calculate the size, set a scale for each triangle of the graph paper. If the quilt will be a baby or wall quilt, it might be better to use a smaller scale. Otherwise, you won't get much design in the small area you have to work with. A king-size bed quilt would go together faster and be in better proportion if the size of the patches were based on a larger scale. If you are particular about the size of a design, you may have to draft pieces, or the math involved will be too complex.

Being in control of the size of the star allows you to keep the points of the star on the top of the bed. If the points were over the edge of the bed, you would not be able to enjoy the whole star. As you design the star, you will set the scale as necessary and add borders, either plain or pieced, to bring the quilt to the desired size.

In diamond patchwork, we measure the perpendicular, or height, of the triangle and not the length of the side. For example, a 9-patch block has three divisions on each side. Using a 2" scale, the block would be 6" square (2" scale times three divisions equals 6"). A 9-patch diamond block has three divisions on each side, but we count rows of equilateral triangles to arrive at the height of the diamond. Using a scale of 2" for each triangle, the length of the diamond would be 12".

Multiplying the scale times the number of rows in the design will only give you the length of the side of the quilt. Measure the side of your triangle and multiply that times the number of triangles across the quilt in your diagram to determine the width of the quilt.

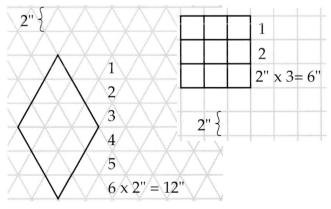

Fig. 24: Calculating Size

Borders

Any star will benefit from the addition of a border. The addition of a border can be simple or challenging. A simple border will certainly complete the top quickly. It is also a wonderful place to show off fancy quilting designs. Include the border in your plans, cutting it lengthwise. Any strips needed for cutting patches for the star can also be cut lengthwise from this fabric.

Framing the quilt with a pieced border will often enhance the star. If you choose to add a pieced border or two, plan to cut the background a little bigger than necessary. The background will later be trimmed to fit the border. Adding a pieced border in this way is easier than having to sew the border to fit the quilt. If your pieced border will place bias at the outside edge of the quilt, stabilize these edges with a plain border, measuring across the middle of the quilt to determine the length.

I have included some border designs you could use. If you would like to design your own border, use the equilateral triangle grid paper, as you did for the star. Keep to the same scale and try to repeat some of the shapes that are in the star. This is not the time to introduce squares and half-square triangles.

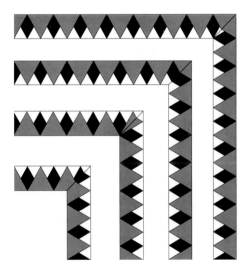

Fig. 26: Different Corners Based On Same Border.

Take a separate sheet of paper and draw up several possible designs. Then hold each one to the drawing of the star and look for compatibility. Watch that the border you choose does not dominate the star.

When I find one I like, I often make up a sample border. Some borders are more work than the star; if I make a sample first, I can be sure I'll be happy with the amount of work the border involves.

When designing a border with equilateral triangle paper, you won't be able to make the design turn the corner. To

Fig. 26: Border Designs.

decide how you want the corners to meet, use the mirrors, this time to reflect a 90° turn. Aim for a pleasing corner from a miter rather than drafting and cutting pieces to fit. Try turning the corner at different points along the border to find the corner that appeals to you the most.

It is easier to fit borders to a square quilt, because all four sides will be made the same length. Pieced borders can be fitted to a rectangular quilt, too. Choose a border with design elements that repeat often. Some borders require reversing the direction of the units for the corners to miter.

Yardage Estimates

Many quilters don't calculate yardage before they purchase it. Perhaps it is more bother than it is worth, or maybe they just don't mind the scraps. When I make a quilt, I usually work with the fabric I already have at home unless one of those fabrics doesn't work. If I am buying fabric for a specific quilt, my estimates are usually generous because I like the scraps and I don't want to be caught short.

Don't be overly concerned about having enough fabric to complete a project. Historically, quilters have not always had the luxury of enough fabric of their choice to complete their quilts and have had to make do with what was at hand. This happens even today as we purchase fabric and store it away for years before finding the right time to use it. If this has happened to you, you may have found that in making substitutions, you have been forced to be a little creative. I hate to hear that a quilt is left unfinished because the quiltmaker ran short of fabric.

If you are purchasing fabric for a particular star, the size of the quilt will suggest how much you need to buy. For instance, a full-size quilt would need about ten yards of fabric. The more piecing in the quilt, the more fabric is taken up in the seams. The number of different fabrics, too, influences how much you will need of any one fabric.

Yardage estimates can be made by using the charts with the cutting directions. The charts show how many units can be cut from a strip. Divide that number into the total number of pieces you need of that shape. This tells you how many strips you need. Multiply the number of strips times the strip width for the amount of fabric needed.

I estimate the yardage for the background by drawing a cutting plan to scale. On graph paper mark off a 43" width of fabric. Draw in background shapes. Include any pieces of background fabric used in the diamonds forming the star and the border. Then calculate the length. When cutting the background or border fabric, always cut the biggest pieces first or you may have to buy more fabric or add unnecessary seams.

Fig. 27: The Width Of Repeats In Border Designs Varies.

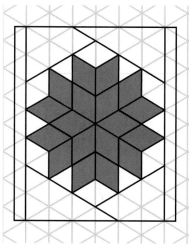

Fig. 28a: Quilt Designs

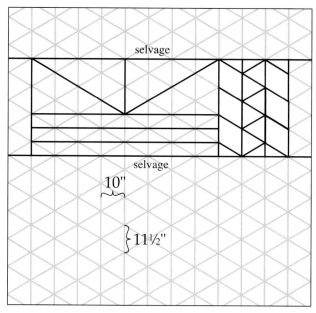

selvage

selvage

10"

11½"

Fig. 28b: Estimating Background Yardage:
11 X 10" = 110"= 3 yds 2".

STAR SAPPHIRE, 80" x 80".

This stunning crystal formed when the Sawtooth pattern was used in a hexagon set. The wider repeat of the border design was better suited to a square quilt.

Chapter 3 ... *Tips for a Smooth Flat Quilt Top*

Before we move on to cutting specific designs, it is important to review some tips for cutting and piecing that will result in a smooth, flat quilt top.

Tools

Being a quilter, you may already have a rotary cutter and mat. Many quilters have them, even if they only use them for cutting borders and sashing. Besides these, you'll also need a clear plastic ruler for measuring and cutting strips and a 60° clear plastic triangle to be used as a master template.

It is important that you note that all 60° triangles are not marked in the same way. This method of template-free cutting is easier to follow when using a triangle that begins measuring at the very tip of the triangle. Other triangles begin measuring within the ¼" seam allowance added to all sides. This makes a difference of ½" in the measurements along the ruled lines. If you use a triangle like that, you will need to subtract ½" from the measurements made using it.

I use the Clearview Triangle® by Sara Nephew. I recommend the 12" triangle for improved accuracy when cutting bigger pieces. If this triangle is not available through your local quilt shop, the address for ordering it is listed in the back of the book.

Rotary Cutting Basics

All the patches, unless they are large background pieces, are cut from strips. To cut a strip accurately, first fold the fabric in half lengthwise, matching selvages. If the fabric wrinkles along the fold, move the top layer of fabric right or left to eliminate the wrinkles. Place the fabric on the mat with the fold closest to you. Place the perpendicular line of the triangle exactly on the fold with the base to the left and near the raw edges. Then place the ruler against the base of the triangle.

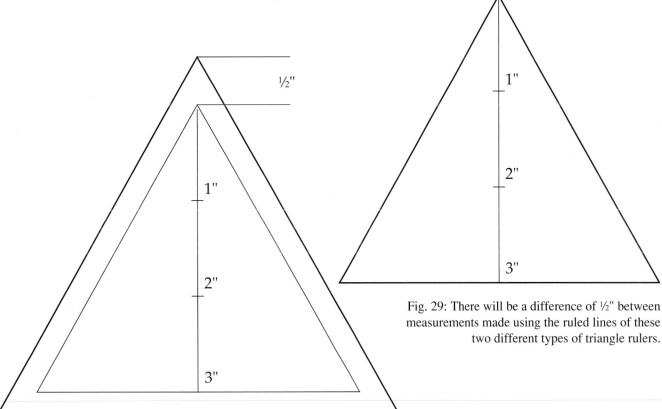

Fig. 29: There will be a difference of ½" between measurements made using the ruled lines of these two different types of triangle rulers.

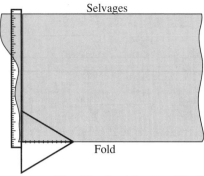

Fig. 30a: Straightening The Edge.

Remove the triangle and take one long cut along the ruler, cleaning and straightening the edge. Fold the fabric in half again, matching the cut edges. A shorter cut will make it easier to control the ruler. Now strips can be measured and cut the required width. If your ruler is not wide enough to cut the strips, use the bottom of the triangle to make up the difference.

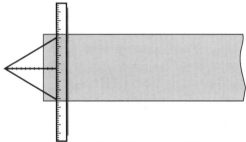

Fig. 30b: Cutting Wide Strips.

After cutting each 18" of fabric, open a strip to make sure it doesn't have "the bends." This waving is caused by the ruler not being lined up exactly perpendicular to the fold. If necessary, open up one fold of the remaining fabric and straighten the edge again, refold and continue cutting. Stay consistent with the side of the markings on the ruler you line up with the fabric. A few threads will make a difference in cutting, as in sewing.

Seams

At a recent workshop I attended, several of the women worked on the same pattern. The combination of different rulers, which side of the black line they used and the width of the seam allowances made a difference of 1½" in the blocks.

This suggests the importance of accurate seam allowances. For patches that will fit together perfectly, it is necessary to sew the seam allowance at the same width it was cut. Check occasionally to see that you are always sewing ¼" seams. (I can't stress enough the importance of accurate ¼" seams.)

Don't trust seam gauges that are screwed down or held in place magnetically. My experience shows they move gradually and cause inaccurate seam widths. The little bit they move is enough to cause problems. It would be better to mark the machine with masking tape or a permanent pen.

Stitch with 12 stitches to the inch. A shorter, stronger stitch will give you more control, as it allows the fabric to travel more slowly through the machine. Be sure to use matching or neutral-color thread. Don't take a chance of ruining your quilt with thread of the wrong color showing through.

Matching Dot To Dot

Matching seam lines exactly will ensure you don't chop off the star points with another seam. Matching dot to dot is the technique I use when I piece, especially when working with points as in the 60° work.

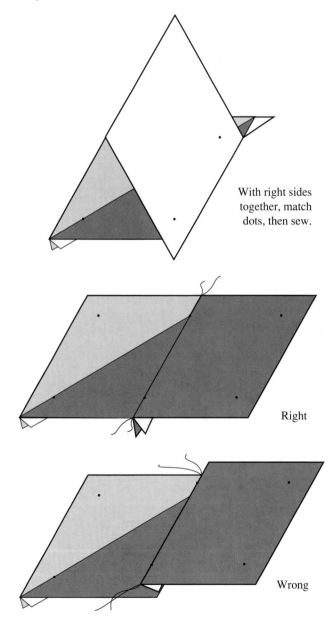

With right sides together, match dots, then sew.

Right

Wrong

Fig. 31: Matching Dots Will Result In Perfectly Aligned patches.

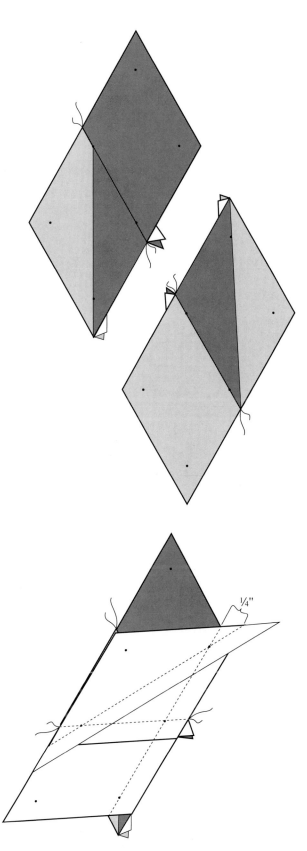

Fig. 32: Using Seam Allowance Tips
As Notches For Aligning Seams.

The dot is the point on the patch where seams intersect with other seams. In machine piecing the line of stitching extends beyond the dots to the edge of the fabric. I visualize the ¼" seams down each side of the patch, and where they meet is where I know the dot is. You might want to mark the dot with an X on the wrong side of the patch.

When matching seams, we have a tendency to just pin where the seams meet between the ends. The more pointed the piece is, the more the presser foot will push it out of shape. You can be assured the seams will match if you pin dot to dot at the end of the seam. You may need to ease in the top piece as you sew.

You will probably find that the pieces will feed straighter and more easily if you start at the end of the seam opposite the point. In this way, you can avoid feeding the point into the hole with the needle. Some designs call for piecing another unit to half-diamonds which have a point at each end. You may trim some of the point in the seam allowance of the half-diamond to reduce bulk and ease handling.

Don't be too hasty to trim the excess seam allowance at the tip of a triangle or diamond. Occasionally, these little tips make wonderful notches for matching up seams.

Order Of Piecing

Some thought should be given to piecing the diamonds in the easiest order possible. Often, the best order will be identical to that of the original square grid patchwork block, only the patches will be at the 60° angle. If you changed a line, moved the mirrors or dropped out the points, you should analyze the new diamond to determine which pieces you will cut and the best piecing order. You may also be able to eliminate unnecessary seams if you combined patches.

In general, you will be sewing patches together into units, then the units into rows and finally, the rows together into diamonds. These pieced diamonds will then be sewn together to form a star.

To assemble a 6-pointed star, first, sew two pieced diamonds together. Press the seam open. Add a third diamond, and press the seam open. Repeat for the other half of the star. Sew the two halves together with one long seam and press it open. When sewing these pieced diamonds together, stop and lockstitch at the dot to allow for setting in the background. When you come to the end of a seam, if you backstitch a few stitches early and then continue to the dot, any stitching that falls in the seam allowance can then easily be removed.

To assemble a 12-pointed star, sew two pieced diamonds together and then a pieced diamond with a background triangle. The straight edge of the triangle should be to the outside of the quilt. Piece these two sections together. These sections of three pieced diamonds can then be treated as diamonds themselves and assembled as the 6-pointed star. The seams of these last sections should stop at the dot to allow for setting in background diamonds.

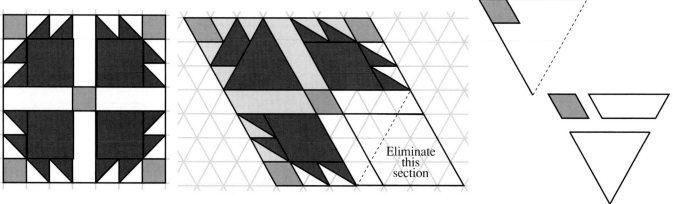

Fig. 33a: Dove In The Window block.

Fig. 33b: Determining Patches To Cut
For Part Of Dove In The Window Block.

Fig. 34: FIREWORKS Design Using Dove In The Window Block.

Handling Bias Edges

As in any patchwork, it is important that you are aware of the bias edges of the fabric. In diamond patchwork, you can't avoid the bias. If handled carefully, bias edges should not be a problem. Following these suggestions should help to prevent the ripples caused by fitting a stretched bias edge to a straight-of-grain edge.

Stretching can occur even before the seams are sewn. Whenever possible, avoid holding the work by a bias edge. Hold it at a seam or along a straight-of-grain edge.

You'll want to support the weight of the piece as it gets bigger. Don't pull on the piece or let it hang from your hands. Place your hands under the work to move it.

Pressing

We can all agree that pressing is important to the appearance of the quilt. Pressing incorrectly is probably the biggest cause of stretched bias edges.

Before cutting any fabric, it should be prewashed to remove excess dye and to preshrink it. Ironing to remove wrinkles will give you a better chance of cutting the fabric accurately. Using spray starch or fabric sizing will stabilize the fabric and aid in preventing distortion.

Ironing can easily distort patches by stretching the bias. This will affect how the patches will fit together. Use a gentle touch with the iron set at cotton. The heat will set the patches apart. It is not necessary to push the iron around to flatten the seam. Any movement of the iron should be in the direction the grain runs.

I prefer finger pressing the shorter seams of the smaller units. To finger press, merely pinch or squeeze the patches apart at the seam. Do not pull on opposite ends of the seam and rub against the edge of the table. I don't even like to see the seam rubbed with a fingernail. If this is done carelessly, the fabric is actually pushed out of place, thereby distorting the pieces.

Press the seam allowances to the same side, in the direction of least resistance. This won't always be towards the dark fabric. If a bit of the dark seam allowance shows through the light patch, the seam allowance can be trimmed.

Press the seam allowances to the same side, in each of the diamonds in the same way. When the diamonds are sewn together, the seams may be ironed open to minimize the lump from so many seams. This will allow the star to lie flatter and make quilting easier.

FIREWORKS, 58" x 62".
The Dove in the Window block makes an interesting star with the points dropped out. The diamond border did an excellent job of enhancing this star.

Chapter 4 ... *T*emplate-*F*ree *C*utting

After converting dozens of blocks to diamonds, I consistently arrived at the same six shapes that can be cut without marking the fabric or using templates. They are: equilateral triangle, half-triangle, diamond, half-diamond, trapezoid and parallelogram. Several of these frequently show up with their matching mirror images. They can be pieced using familiar template-free methods.

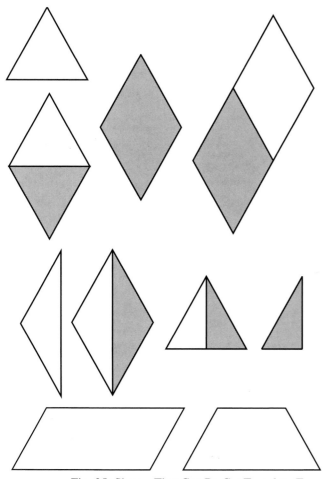

Fig. 35: Shapes That Can Be Cut Template-Free.

Template-free cutting will speed up the quiltmaking process. This does not mean that the piecing will be faster. Enjoy your piecing and take care to be accurate.

If you are familiar with template-free cutting methods, then you are aware that patches are cut from strips of fabric. The basic rule to determine the strip width is the finished measurement of the patch plus the width of the seam allowance. The finished measurement is determined by the scale we set for each triangle of the graph paper. First count the number of rows of triangles in the patch and multiply by

the scale. Always add the seam allowance last. The amount to add for the seam allowance is determined by the shape being cut. This will equal the width to cut your strips from which the patches will be cut. Examples will be shown using a 2" scale.

Equilateral Triangles

If you were to draft an equilateral triangle and add a ¼" seam allowance to each side, you would see that you have actually added ¾" to the triangle's perpendicular measurement. So the strip width to cut a triangle is the finished measurement plus ¾".

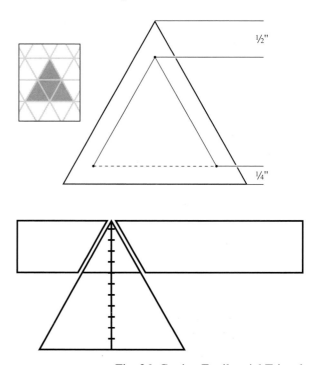

Fig. 36: Cutting Equilaterial Triangles.

For example, let's look at a triangle two rows high. Multiply two rows by 2" scale to equal 4" and add ¾" seam allowance. The strip width is 4¾". Once the strip is cut, place the triangle ruler on the strip, matching the ruled line for the correct size triangle with the edge of fabric. The point on the ruler should not extend beyond the opposite edge of the fabric. Cut on each side of the triangle ruler. For successive cuts, the triangle only needs to be slid over until the side of the triangle ruler comes to the point of the last triangle. Cut on both sides of the triangle ruler again and continue across the strip.

Sandwich Pieced Equilateral Triangles

Quite often, where there is one equilateral triangle, there will be a matching triangle. They correspond to half-square triangle units in traditional patchwork blocks. These can be cut template free also.

Using two different fabrics, cut strips the same width as for individual triangles. With right sides together, sew ¼" away from both long edges of the strips. Then cut the strips the same as for triangles, matching the ruled line for correct triangle size. Clip stitching where the tips are sewn together and finger press. At this point all four sides will be bias.

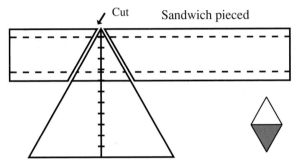

Fig. 37: Cutting Sandwich Pieced Equilateral Triangles.

Triangles

Finished Perpendicular	Strip Width	Per 42" Strip	Side Length
1½	2¼	29	1¾
2	2¾	25	2⅜
2½	3¼	21	2¹⁵⁄₁₆
3	3¾	17	3½
4	4¾	13	4¹¹⁄₁₆
4½	5¼	13	5³⁄₁₆
5	5¾	11	5¹³⁄₁₆
6	6¾	9	7
7½	8¼	7	8⅛
8	8¾	7	9¼
10	10¾	6	11⁹⁄₁₆

Fig. 38

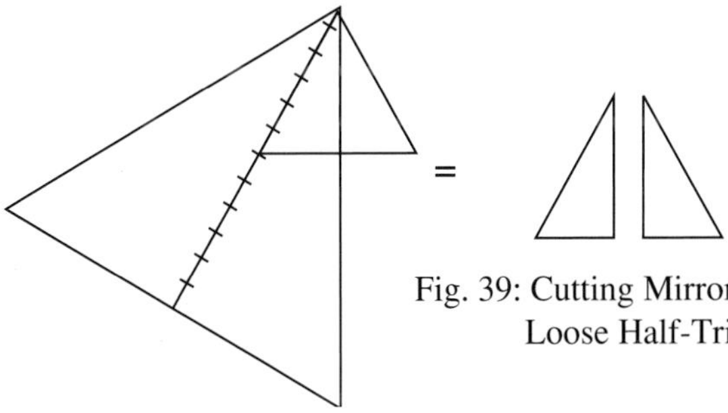

Loose Half-Triangles

When a ¼" seam is added all around a half-triangle, we see that 1¼" is added to its height. If the design uses its mirror image, it is a simple matter of cutting triangles 1¼" larger than the finished measurement and then bisecting them.

For example, a half-triangle only one row high has a finished perpendicular of 2". Add the 1¼" seam allowance and cut triangles at 3¼". Then bisect them. To bisect a triangle, match the perpendicular line of the triangle ruler to an edge of the triangle and cut it in half.

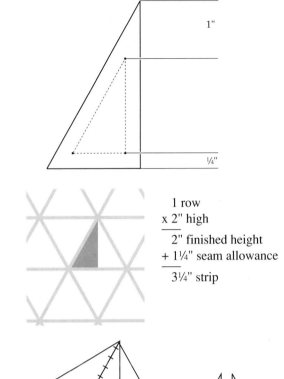

1 row
x 2" high
2" finished height
+ 1¼" seam allowance
3¼" strip

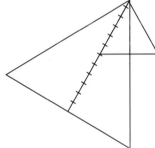

Fig. 39: Cutting Mirror Image Loose Half-Triangles.

If the design uses identical half-triangles (all cut in the same direction), then start with a strip, half of the width of the base of the cut triangle (including the 1¼") or according to the chart below.

Half-Triangles

Finished Perpen.	Strip Width	Rect. Length	Per 42" Strip
1½	1⅝	2¾	30
2	1⅞	3¼	24
2½	2¼	3¾	22
3	2½	4¼	18
4	3¼	5¼	16
4½	3⅜	5¾	14
5	3⅝	6¼	12
6	4¼	7¼	10
7½	5⅛	8¾	8
8	5¼	9¼	8

Fig. 40

For a half-triangle with a finished perpendicular of 2", cut strips 1⅞" wide. Then cut into rectangles 3¼" long. Do not just cut these rectangles diagonally. Rather, to be accurate, line the perpendicular of the ruler up with the long edge of the rectangle. The point should not extend beyond the fabric. Cut the 30° angle. Reverse what is left of the rectangle and repeat. A sliver of fabric may remain because the strip width may be little wider than necessary to avoid having to cut ¹⁄₁₆ of an inch. Cut all of the rectangles at the same angle.

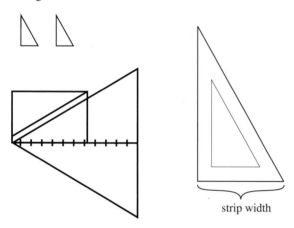

Fig. 41: Cutting Identical Half-Triangles.

In some designs there may be matching half-triangle units. These can be sandwich pieced also. Refer to the same chart for strip width. Sew two strips, right sides together, ¼" away from each long edge. Subcut into rectangles then half-triangles, matching the perpendicular of the triangle to the raw edge. Carefully remove the few stitches holding the unit closed and finger press open. For designs using mirror image matching half-triangle units, cut half of the rectangles by matching the perpendicular to the opposite edge of the strip to yield half-triangles cut at the correct angle. Flipping the strip over half-way through will also result in half-triangles cut at the proper angle.

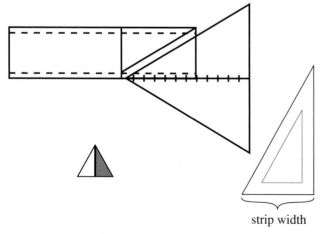

Fig. 42: Cutting Matching Half-Triangles.

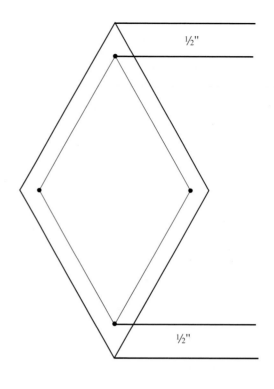

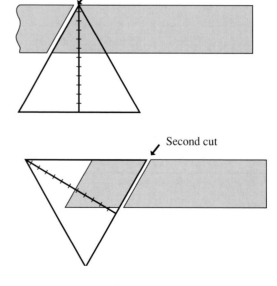

Fig. 43: Cutting Diamonds.

Diamonds

When you draft a diamond with a ¼" seam on each side, you add 1" to its height (Fig. 43). The strip width is half of the diamond's cut perpendicular measurement. For example, a 4" finished diamond equals a 5" cut diamond which uses a 2½" strip.

Another way to calculate the strip width is to count the number of rows between parallel sides of the diamond, multiply by the scale and add ½" to allow for ¼" seams.

Diamonds

Finished Perpendicular	Cut Perpendicular	Strip Width	Per 42" Strip
3	4	2	16
4	5	2½	13
5	6	3	11
6	7	3½	9
8	9	4½	7
9	10	5	6
10	11	5½	5
12	13	6½	5

Fig. 44

Cut a 60° angle off the left end of the strip. For the next cut, tip the triangle ruler on its left side and use the back end to measure and cut the diamond the same length that the strip is wide. By doing so you can keep two lines on the ruler matched to two edges of fabric. This will ensure accuracy.

When two diamonds are to be sewn together as in a 4-patch, you can quickly and accurately piece them in the same manner as you would a 4-patch of squares.

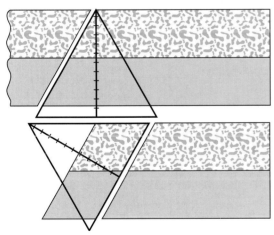

Fig. 45: Cutting Double Diamonds.

Calculate the strip width and sew the two strips of contrasting fabric together. Cut a 60° angle off the left end as you do for diamonds. Again, using the back end of the triangle, subcut into sections the same width as the individual strips.

Loose Half-Diamonds

When a half-diamond is drafted with a ¼" seam, two inches are added to its overall height. First calculate the half-diamond's cut perpendicular measurement. For example, a 4" half-diamond equals a 6" cut half-diamond. Measure the width of the cut half-diamond to find the strip width. A little extra may be allowed. You may refer to the chart for the required strip width.

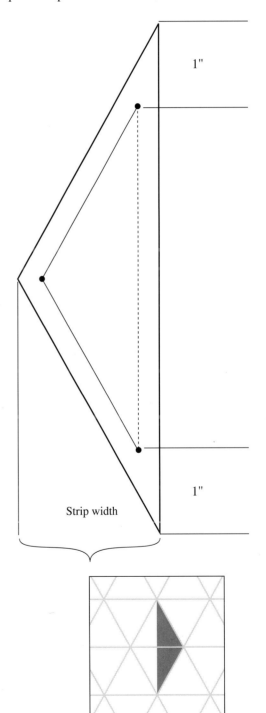

1"

1"

Strip width

Fig. 46a: Cutting Loose Half-Diamonds.

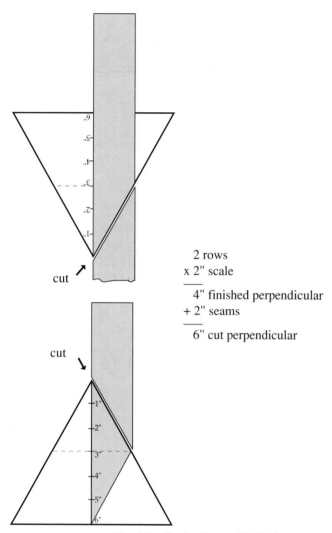

2 rows
x 2" scale

4" finished perpendicular
+ 2" seams

6" cut perpendicular

cut

cut

Fig. 46b: Cutting Loose Half-Diamonds.

Half-Diamonds

Finished Perpendicular	Cut Perpendicular	Strip Width*	Per 42" Strip
3	5	1½	15
4	6	1¾	12
5	7	2⅛	10
6	8	2⅜	9
8	10	2⅞	7
9	11	3¼	5
10	12	3½	5

* For *strip pieced* half-diamond units, cut strips ¼" wider than stated.

Fig. 47

With the ruler upside down, match the perpendicular line of the triangle to the left edge of fabric and the point of the triangle to the selvage edge of the strip. Cut a 30° angle off the bottom of the strip. Turn the triangle ruler around. Match the perpendicular of the triangle ruler to the long edge of the fabric and the measurement of the cut half-diamond at the point of the 30° angle. One more point to match to ensure accuracy is the edge of the fabric cut at the angle, which should meet the ruler at half the size of the half-diamond. Keeping the triangle ruler right side up, alternately match the perpendicular of the ruler to the left and right edges of the strip. Cutting will alternate to the left and the right of the ruler. Or, flipping the strip over after each cut will enable you to always cut off the right side of the triangle.

If the tip of the seam allowance is cut off the next half-diamond, matching the edge of fabric cut at the angle to half the size of the half-diamond will be accurate.

Sandwich Pieced Matching Half-Diamond Units

Matching half-diamonds come up frequently in these designs. They also correspond to half-square triangle units in traditional square patchwork. They can be quickly pieced in any of the same ways. I present two ways, each having advantages.

I use sandwich piecing when I only need about a dozen units. There is very little waste. You may need as little as one strip of each fabric.

Cut strip width according to the chart or the width of the cut half-diamond. With right sides together, seam ¼" away on each side of the strip. Cut as for loose half-diamonds.

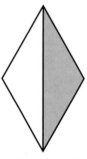

Fig. 48: Sandwich Pieced Matching Half-Diamond Unit.

Strip Pieced Matching Half-Diamond Units

To quickly piece these pairs, I like to use the strip method. This method has several advantages over other techniques often used. (1) It is easier to press the bigger strips than little pairs of half-diamonds. (2) Better accuracy is achieved because you cut after the seam is taken. (3) The pieces will not become distorted when pressed. (4) The points will not need to be trimmed. I prefer this technique when the pattern requires several dozen of these units.

Calculate the size of the matching half-diamond unit you need. Find this size in the chart. Read across the chart to find the strip width. For this method, add ¼" to the width the chart gives. The resulting strip will be a little wider than necessary. The excess will be trimmed away as the units are cut. Cut strips this size from each fabric used. Sew the strips together with ¼" seams, alternating the fabrics. Sew at least four strips together. If your design calls for several combinations of colors you may be able to sew them all together so there is less waste. Press the seams together toward the dark fabric. Line up the desired diamond size (the cut size of the matching half-diamond unit) and the perpendicular line on the ruler with the seam and cut on each side of the triangle.

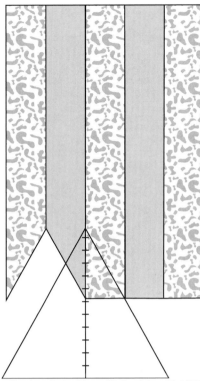

Fig. 49b: Cutting Strip Pieced Matching Half-Diamonds.

Turn the piece around and cut again, matching the perpendicular line with the seam and the diamond size with the point. Cut one diamond off at a time. The diamonds may all be cut off before they are turned around for trimming.

If you are tempted to cut a strip off and then cut off diamonds, caution must be used to keep the strip cut accurately at a 30° angle to the seams. For a little insurance cut the strip a little wider and trim a little more.

Parallelograms

The strip width for parallelograms is the finished perpendicular plus ½" (to allow for ¼" seams). They are cut the same way as the diamonds, only longer. The length is determined by multiplying the number of rows of triangles in the graph paper times the scale plus a ½" for seam allowances. For example, a parallelogram 2" wide requires a 2½" wide strip. Graphed at two rows long, the parallelogram would be cut 4½" long.

If you want all the parallelograms cut at the same angle, unfold the strip before cutting. Check that the parallelograms will be cut at the proper angle for your design. If cutting a 60° angle off the left side of the strip when it is face up would result in the wrong angle, then turn the fabric over. Some designs call for half of the parallelograms to be cut in reverse. In that case leave your strip folded as you cut.

Cut a 60° angle off the left side of the strip. Tip the top of the triangle ruler to the left and use the back end of the

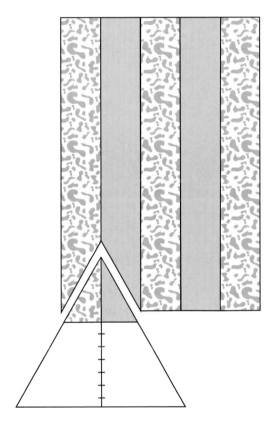

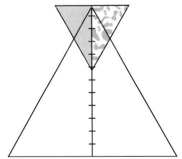

Fig. 49a: Cutting Strip Pieced Matching Half-Diamonds.

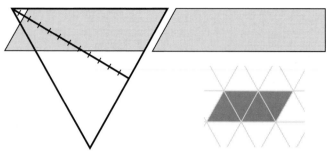

Fig. 50: Cutting Parallelograms.

triangle ruler to measure and cut the parallelogram. Matching two sides of the triangle to two edges of fabric will improve accuracy.

Trapezoids

Trapezoids are cut from strips with ½" added to the finished perpendicular measurement. Notice that the trapezoid is the base of a larger imaginary triangle. Calculate the size of that triangle and cut (be sure to use the formula which adds ¾"). Matching the edge of fabric with the base of the imaginary cut triangle, cut on both sides of the triangle. For the next piece, move on down the strip, but flip the ruler and match its side to the edge of the fabric.

In this example, the strip width would be 2½". The imaginary triangle cut would be 8¾".

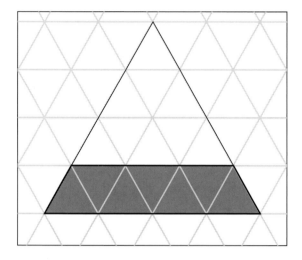

1 row	4 row
x 2" scale	x 2" scale
2" finished width	8" imaginary triangle
+ ½" seam allowance	+ ¾" seam allowance
2½" strip width	8¾" cut imaginary triangle

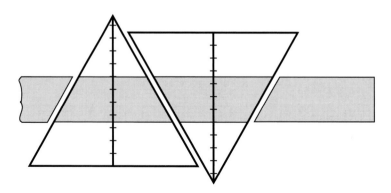

Fig. 51: Cutting Trapezoids.

Chapter 5 ... *Background and Borders*

The size of your background pieces will to some extent determine the size of the quilt. Remember to add extra if you will be fitting pieced borders. Be careful that you don't add too much or the star will appear lost in space. It would be better to add another border. Cut the background pieces first so you'll be sure to have enough if you need the same fabric for piecework.

The Six-Pointed Star Background

Straighten the edge of background fabric. Fold it with selvages parallel. The amount between selvage and fold should equal half the height of the pieced diamonds plus 2" to float the star. Cut the single layer of fabric along the selvage. For piece A, place the perpendicular line of the ruler on the straightened edge with the point of the triangle at the selvage. Cut a 30° angle. Extend the cut to the fold, using your ruler. To measure the length to cut pieces B and E, fold the 120° angle in half by bringing the edge just cut to the fold. Align the cut edge with the fold and mark where the tip of the cut edge hits it. Unfold the 120° angle. The next cut is perpendicular to the fold at the mark just made. Separate

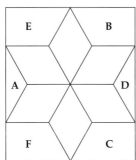

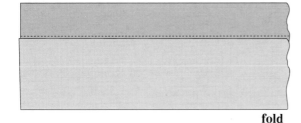

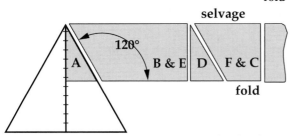

Fig. 52: Cutting Background pieces for 6-pointed stars.

pieces B and E by cutting apart at the fold. Repeat the same steps for pieces D, C and F, as shown in Fig. 52.

If you are fitting a pieced border or making a square top, the perpendicular of the triangle ruler should be placed to the right of the straightened edge when you are cutting background pieces. Use your diagram to estimate how much. Use your ruler to keep the base of the triangle parallel to the fold.

The background pieces of the 6-pointed star will have to be set in. Insert the side half-diamonds first. Check the illustration for the proper placement of pieces B, C, E and F. Remember, you are still working with bias edges. At this point, to prevent either edge from stretching, spread the star and background pieces on the table. Match and pin the dot and edges before sewing. Sew one seam at a time, taking it out from the machine after each seam. It doesn't matter if you sew toward the corner or away from it. What is most important is that the sewing does not extend into the seam allowance. Sew only to the end of the stitching line on your star diamonds. The background fabric will be larger than necessary. When all background pieces have been set in, seam the extra fabric in adjacent background pieces, sewing from each star point out to the cut edge. When all seams have been sewn, you can trim the background edge so the block fits your chosen borders or finished quilt size.

Twelve-Pointed Star Background

If the background pieces for the 12-pointed star are drawn in the diagram it is easy to cut them to the same scale. The triangles will have been used when assembling the star. The diamonds will need to be set in. The dotted line in the illustration on page 44 gives you the option of a smaller quilt. You may need to make the background the larger size to fit the border to the quilt or bring the quilt to the desired size.

To cut the large outside half-triangles, straighten the edge perpendicular to the fold. Remove the selvages. Open the fabric to a single layer. Calculate the finished perpendicular plus 1¼" required for half-triangles. Measure the lengthwise edge of the fabric and place the perpendicular line of the triangle on it. Cut a 30° angle, extending it with your ruler. Use this piece as a template to cut out the opposite triangle. For the last two pieces, turn the fabric over to cut them at the proper angle. See Figure 28 for cutting layout and estimating background-fabric yardage.

Trimming The Background

You should trim the star background before adding a plain border. You'll have nice, square corners and sides of equal length. Directions for trimming the background when adding a pieced border follow.

Fold the quilt top in half when trimming or the star will not be centered. Match the star points and secure with pins. Cut parallel to the fold, at least ¼" beyond the star points. Unpin and refold in the other direction for the opposite two sides.

In some of the quilts I accented the corners of the plain borders. Corners are 90° angles, so three half-triangles (30° each) will fill the corners of the quilt and add a little interest. The center half-triangle will need to be cut bigger, as shown in Fig. 54. Add the side half-triangles by matching the dot at the point. The center triangle can be squared off using the ruler and rotary cutter; no template will be necessary.

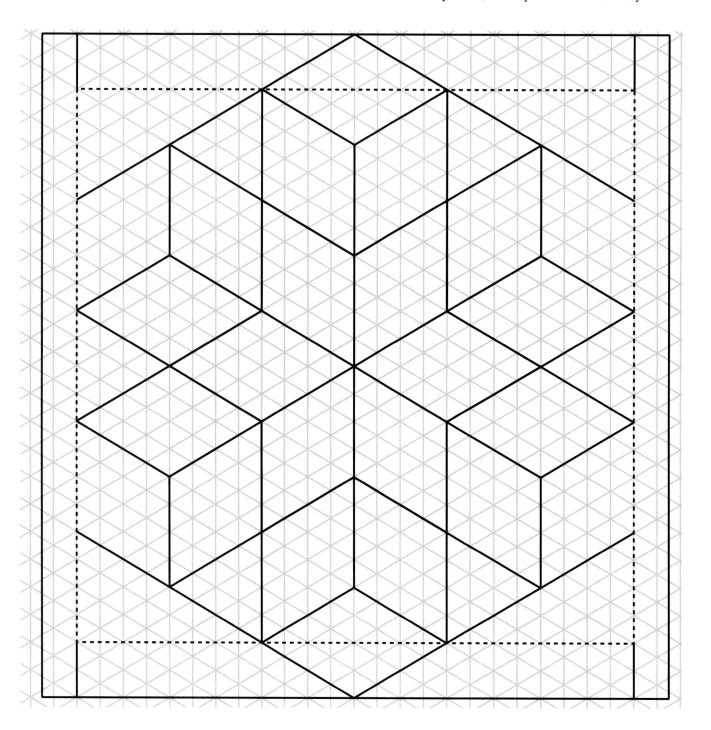

Fig. 53: Design showing a background for a 12-pointed star (with 4 divisions across each pieced diamond).

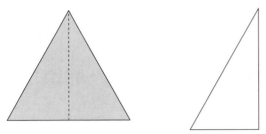

Fig. 54: Cut Three 30° Triangles For Border Corners.

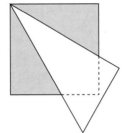

Fig. 55: Trim The Center Triangle
Using A Ruler And Rotary Cutter.

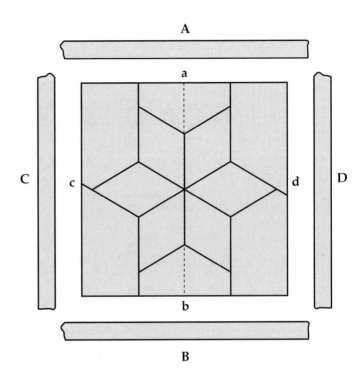

Fig. 56: Fitting Borders To Background.

Sew the borders on the two long sides. Add the corner pieces to the borders, which have been cut the length of the short side. Sew these last borders to the quilt top. Of course, the borders may be mitered in the usual manner.

Fitting Pieced Borders To The Quilt

If you're using a border stripe or making a pieced border, estimate the length of the borders based on your diagram; then make them a little longer to allow for the miter. After the borders are pieced, measure and trim the background for a perfect fit. Do not sew on any borders until all sides are measured and trimmed.

Following Fig. 56, fold the star in half along the broken line, matching side c to d. Pin matching star points to prevent shifting and ensure accuracy. Measure the inside length of borders A and B from dot to dot. Dots should be marked where the miter will begin at each end. Plan the placement of these dots so the border corners will look matched, with the miter beginning at an identical or comparable place at each end. Trim sides c and d, (parallel to the fold) so that from fold to cut the piece measures half of the inside length of the border plus ¼" seam allowance. You only need to add ¼" because the star is folded. This cut will shorten sides a and b to equal the length of the border.

If the quilt is square, refold the star in half the other way and measure and cut the same amount. If a rectangular quilt is desired, measure borders D and C. Refold the star in half the other way. Pin the star points to keep it from shifting. Trim sides a and b to fit the measurement of the other border pieces.

If the background was not cut big enough to trim away or if you would be cutting away the points of the star, then you may add strips of background fabric. You might also consider adding a border of another fabric before the pieced border. The width of this first border does not need to be the same on all four sides. You could plan for a pillow tuck here.

When adding the border to the quilt, match the centers, corners and quarter way points. Using a walking foot, lockstitch ¼" from the corner to allow for the miter.

Mitering Corners

With right side up, pin one piece of the border to the ironing board in the area of the mitering seam line. At a 45° angle, fold under the corner of another border piece. Match its raw edges and border design to those of the first piece. Check the squareness of the corner and the angle with the 45° angle on your ruler. Press the fold.

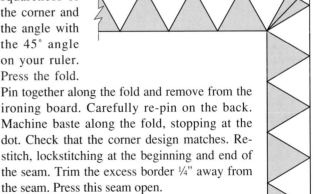

Pin together along the fold and remove from the ironing board. Carefully re-pin on the back. Machine baste along the fold, stopping at the dot. Check that the corner design matches. Re-stitch, lockstitching at the beginning and end of the seam. Trim the excess border ¼" away from the seam. Press this seam open.

Fig. 57: To Miter The Corners, Fold Under On A 45° Angle.
Match Seams And Press.

COUNTRY CHRISTMAS, 52" x 60".
Subtraction and addition techniques were applied to the Cajun Spice block from *Judy Martin's Ultimate Book of Quilt Block Patterns*. The colors contributed to an already "Christmas" look.

Chapter 6 ... *Quilting and Design*

The quilt top is done. Now comes the task of preparing it for quilting. Before marking or basting the quilt top, any dark threads on the back of it which might show through a light patch should be clipped away. The same goes for any excess seam allowance such as where patches are pressed toward the light or the little ears extend beyond the seam allowance. You may have taken care of these as you were piecing, but this is your last chance–so I recommend you check your quilt top to prevent disappointment later. If necessary, press the quilt top one last time before marking for quilting.

"Which quilting design should I use?" is a question I often hear about any quilt. I hope you realize there is no right or wrong quilting design to choose. Do what pleases you. The quilt is your design, including the quilting.

Quilting a 6-pointed star doesn't have to be different from quilting any other star. The star can be quilted in a traditional manner, either in the ditch or ¼" away from the seams. This can be done around each patch or around patches of the same fabric that touch. Marking the quilting design around the star will not be necessary if you use ¼" masking tape as a guide.

The quilting design you choose can create an optical illusion of more piecing or sharper angles in the piecing. You can also emphasize the illusion of curves in your piecing by quilting curves.

Lately, many quilters are disregarding the seams and superimposing an unrelated quilting design over the patchwork or whole top. This may be done to set the mood or create texture or rhythm in the design. Or it may be done to make frame or machine quilting easier.

One way of trying different quilting designs is to sketch some on tracing paper which has been placed over a colored diagram of your star. This is easier than actually quilting a few lines and then ripping the stitches out if you don't like

them. Worse yet, would be to quilt it all in a manner that doesn't enhance the piece and leaves you feeling dissatisfied.

When deciding on the quilting design for the background area, you can keep a traditional look to your quilt by using a feathered design or one of the other commercial quilting stencils available. Try to use a design which repeats six times around rather than eight. Should you still need to fill in background area, crosshatching will work well. If you choose to quilt diamonds in the background, use the same scale as for the patchwork. Start marking off the edge of the pieced diamonds.

I like to quilt the background with rays of light or star shine. These should radiate outward from the center. I've also quilted sparks in the background, but you might prefer little stars in the sky behind the star.

There are many beautiful quilting stencils available for borders. Since much of your quilt has been of your own design, you may choose to design the border quilting, too.

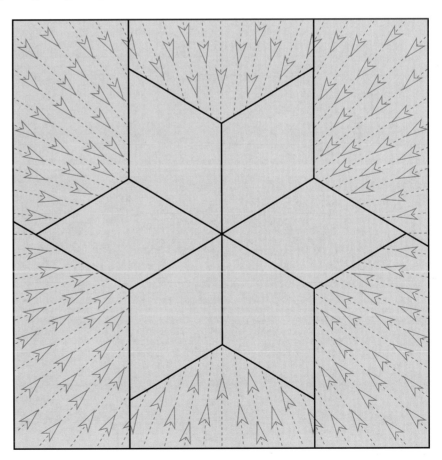

Fig. 58a: Background Quilting Design.

Fig. 58b: Background
Quilting Design

Fig. 58c: Background
Quilting Design

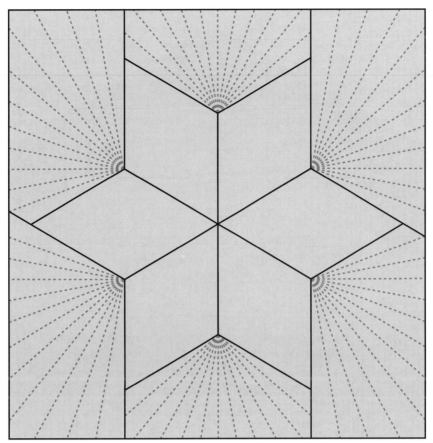

Fig. 58d: Background Quilting Design

BLUE FACETED DIAMOND, 40" x 46", Pat Titus.
Pat's flair for designing is evident in this striking quilt. The pieced background diamonds are based on the same Road to Oklahoma pattern used for the star.

THE SHINING, 38" x 46".

AUTUMN IN THE PINES, 39"x 44".
These three stars are based on the Double X pattern. Notice the similarity to the Anvil pattern.

SATURDAY'S STAR, 27" x 31"

ALIEN STAR FLOWER, 72"x 76".
This glowing flower borrowed lines from Gentleman's Fancy. For more possibilities with this pattern see page 25.

TWILIGHT IN REEDSBURG, 39" x 44".
A summer sky at sunset was the inspiration for the colors in this quilt design using Double X -2.

PEACH CHABLIS, 27" x 31", Pat Titus.
The Grape Basket takes on a new look in this hexagon set by Pat. The colors were used to meet the Wisconsin Quilters challenge.

AMETHYST BROOCH, 45" x 50".
The colors in this quilt were inspired by the paisley fabric used in the border. Subtaction and addition were both used on the Union Square block to create this gem.

VAPOR LIGHT, 43" x 48".
The Picket Fence pattern converted to diamonds resulted in this simple star.

RIBBONS AND LACE, 64" x 64", Sue Bong.
Sue used the Cross and Crown block to design this lovely delicate star.

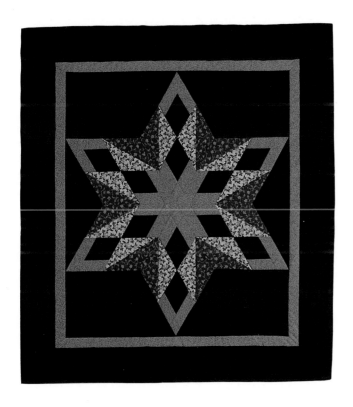

 **STAR OF CHRISTMAS, 36" x 42",**
Gayle Bielanski.
Gayle chose the Chirstmas Star pattern to
make an attractive star.

 **FRIENDSHIP STAR, 38" x 42",**
Gayle Bielanski.
This wallhanging was successful at
developing the friendship of the artist and
the author and of meeting a guild
challenge. Gayle used the Tail of
Benjamin's Kite pattern for this class
project.

 **LET FREEDOM RING, 36" x 40",**
Gayle Bielanski.
The flags in the corner add to the patriotic
theme in this quilt designed using the
Hovering Hawks pattern, also by Gayle
Bielanski.

SOUTHERN BREEZES, 28" x 32",
Gayle Bielanski.
Fabric for the Hoffman challenge was the inspiration for this quilt. Here rectangles were formed when the Centennial 2 block was transformed into a diamond. The triangle chart shows the length of the side or the finished width of the rectangle.

SWALLOWS IN FLIGHT, 27" x 31",
Gayle Bielanski.
The Swallow block in the 1½" scale makes this striking star suitable for repeating across a full size quilt.

Chapter 7 ... *Templates*

These are the templates for diamond blocks designed by the techniques presented in this book. The templates are grouped by scale. Templates from different scales should not be mixed in one project.

Templates include seam lines and cutting lines. Use the line that is compatible with your method of quiltmaking you are using (hand or machine). Trace the templates onto template plastic. If you are tracing onto paper, glue the paper to cardboard before cutting out the template.

Do not photocopy the templates. Accuracy will be lost along the spine of the book. Photocopies might also distort the template at just one end of the page.

If desired, templates can be combined to eliminate unnecessary seams. To do this, trace around the seam line of the first template. Then match seams to the second template, overlapping seam allowances. Trace around the seams of the second template. Add seam allowances to the combined patch.

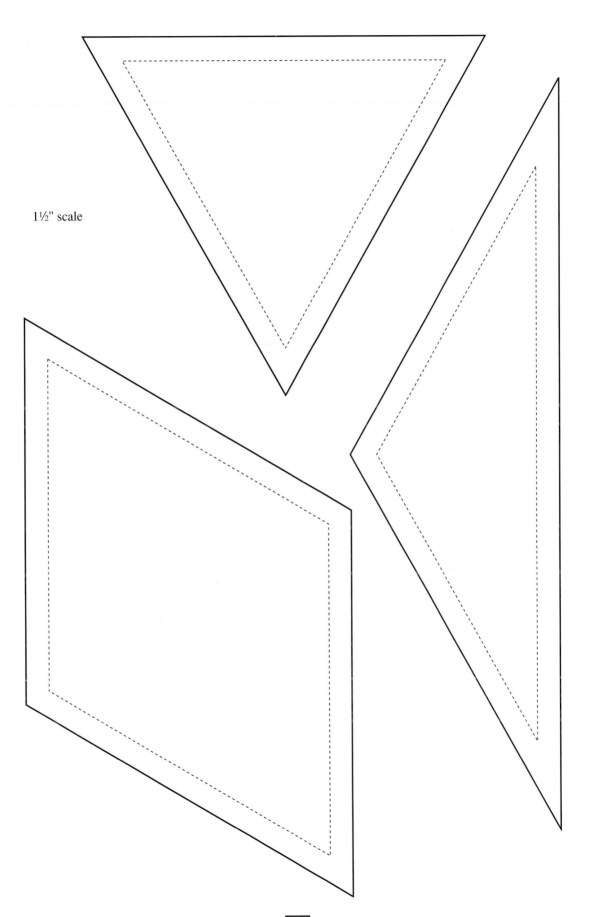

1½" scale

1½" scale

1½" scale

2" scale

2" scale

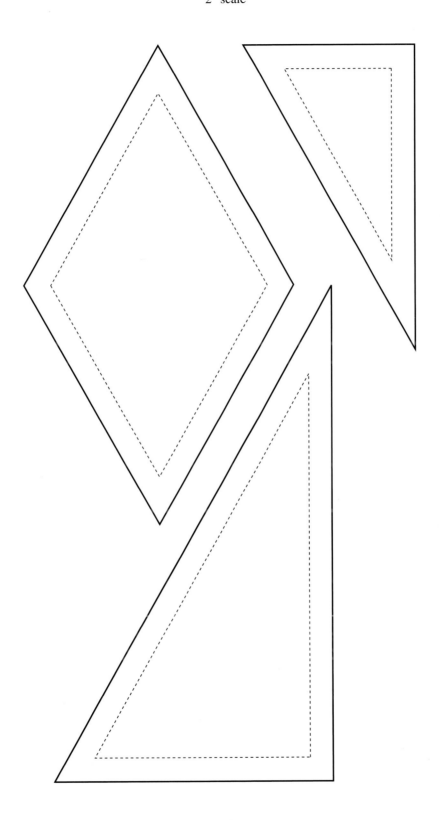

2" scale

2" scale

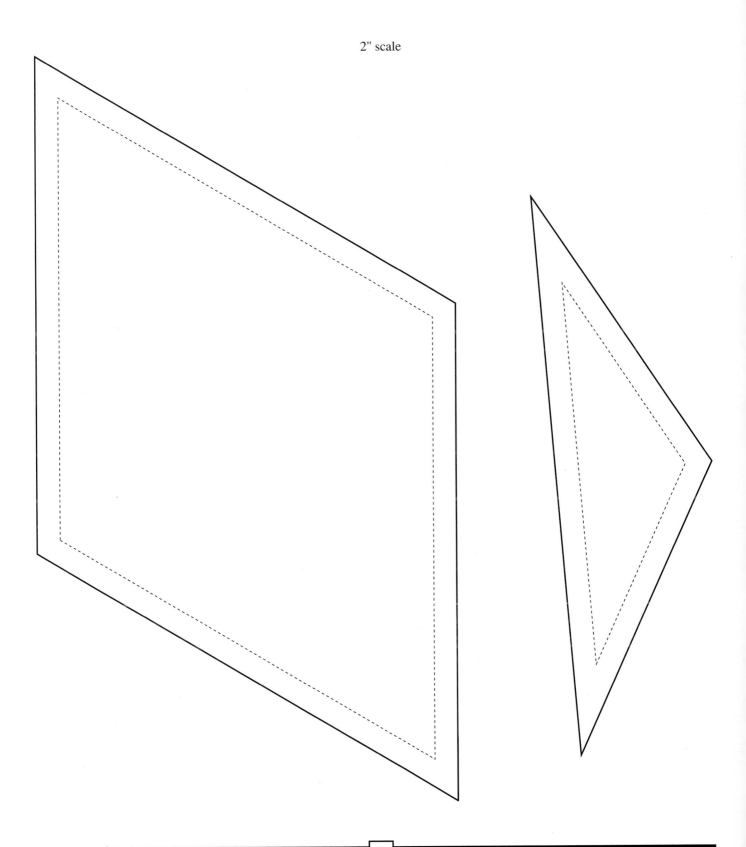

2" scale

2½" scale

2½" scale

2½" scale

2½" scale

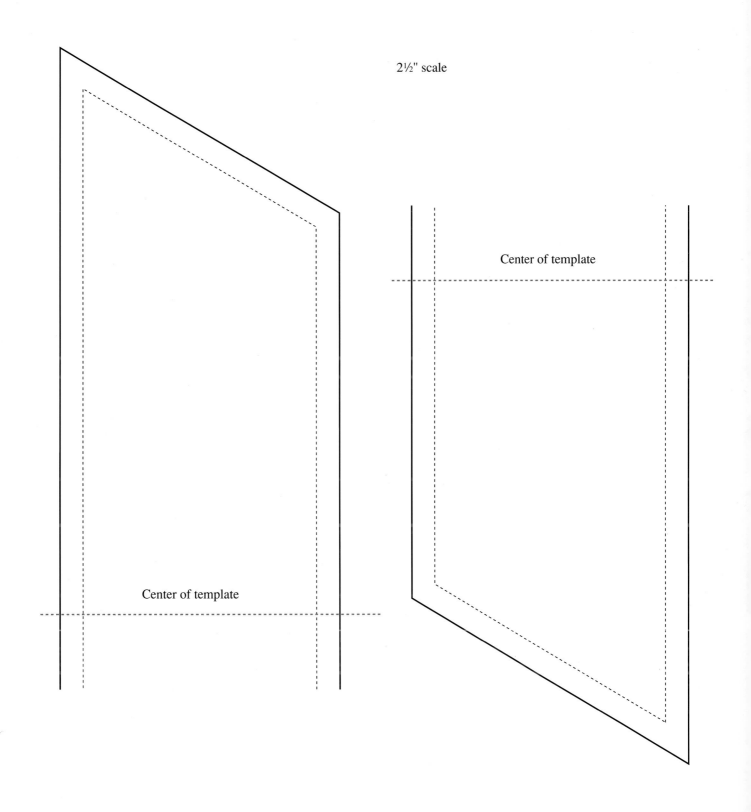

2½" scale

Center of template

Center of template

*B*ibliography

Beyer, Jinny. *The Quilter's Album of Blocks and Borders*. McLean, VA: EPM Publications, Inc., 1980.

Beyer, Jinny. *The Art and Technique of Medallion Quilts*. McLean, VA: EPM Publications, Inc., 1982.

Gutcheon, Jeffrey. *Diamond Patchwork*. Lafayette, CA: C & T Publishing, 1982.

Malone, Maggie. *1001 Patchwork Designs*. New York: Sterling Publishing Co., Inc., 1982.

Martin, Judy. *Judy Martin's Ultimate Book of Quilt Block Patterns*. Denver: Crosley-Griffith Publishing Co., 1988.

Nephew, Sara. *Stars and Flowers: Three Sided Patchwork*. Snohomish, WA: Clearview Triangle, 1989.

Supplies

Clearview Triangles are available from Clearview Triangle Tools, 8311 180th St. S.E., Snohomish, WA 98290.

Graffix equilaterial triangle grid paper is available from Lubisco Studios, P.O. Box 2, Bradley Beach, NJ 07720.

Mirror Magic is available from Great American Quilt Factory, 8970 E. Hampden, Denver CO. 80231 or phone 1-303-740-6206.

American Quilter's Society

dedicated to publishing books for today's quilters

The following AQS publications are currently available:

• **American Beauties: Rose & Tulip Quilts**
by Gwen Marston & Joe Cunningham
#1907: AQS, 1988, 96 pages, softbound, $14.95

• **America's Pictorial Quilts** by Caron L. Mosey
#1662: AQS, 1985, 112 pages, hardbound, $19.95

• **Applique Designs: My Mother Taught Me to Sew**
by Faye Anderson
#2121: AQS, 1990, 80 pages, softbound, $12.95

• **Arkansas Quilts: Arkansas Warmth**
Arkansas Quilter's Guild, Inc.
#1908: AQS, 1987, 144 pages, hardbound, $24.95

• **The Art of Hand Applique** by Laura Lee Fritz
#2122: AQS, 1990, 80 pages, softbound, $14.95

• **...Ask Helen More About Quilting Designs** by Helen Squire
#2099: AQS, 1990, 54 pages, 17 x 11, spiral-bound, $14.95

• **Award-Winning Quilts & Their Makers:**
The Best of AQS Shows – 1985-1987 edited by Victoria Faoro
#2207: AQS, 1991, 232 pages, softbound, $19.95

• **Classic Basket Quilts** by Elizabeth Porter and Marianne Fons
#2208: AQS, 1991, 128 pages, softbound, $16.95

• **A Collection of Favorite Quilts** by Judy Florence
#2119 AQS, 1990, 136 pages, softbound, $18.95

• **Dear Helen, Can You Tell Me?**
...all about quilting designs by Helen Squire
#1820: AQS, 1987, 56 pages, 17 x 11, spiral-bound, $12.95

• **Dyeing & Overdyeing of Cotton Fabrics** by Judy Mercer Tescher
#2030: AQS, 1990, 54 pages, softbound, $9.95

• **Flavor Quilts for Kids to Make: Complete Instructions for Teaching Children To Dye, Decorate & Sew Quilts**
by Jennifer Amor
#2356, AQS, 1991, 120 pages., softbound, $12.95

• **Fun & Fancy Machine Quiltmaking** by Lois Smith
#1982: AQS, 1989, 144 pages, softbound, $19.95

• **Gallery of American Quilts: 1849-1988**
#1938: AQS, 1988, 128 pages, softbound, $19.95

• **Gallery of American Quilts 1860-1989: Book II**
#2129: AQS, 1990, 128 pages, softbound, $19.95

• **The Grand Finale: A Quilter's Guide to Finishing Projects**
by Linda Denner
#1924: AQS, 1988, 96 pages, softbound, $14.95

• **Heirloom Miniatures** by Tina M. Gravatt
#2097: AQS, 1990, 64 pages, softbound, $9.95

• **Home Study Course in Quiltmaking**
by Jeannie M. Spears
#2031: AQS, 1990, 240 pages, softbound, $19.95

• **Infinite Stars** by Gayle Bong
#2283: AQS, 1992, 72 pages, softbound, $12.95

• **The Ins and Outs: Perfecting the Quilting Stitch**
by Patricia J. Morris
#2120: AQS, 1990, 96 pages, softbound, $9.95

• **Irish Chain Quilts: A Workbook of Irish Chains & Related Patterns** by Joyce B. Peaden
#1906: AQS, 1988, 96 pages, softbound, $14.95

• **Marbling Fabrics for Quilts: A Guide for Learning & Teaching**
by Kathy Fawcett and Carol Shoaf
#2206: AQS, 1991, 72 pages, softbound, $12.95

• **Missouri Heritage Quilts** by Bettina Havig
#1718: AQS, 1986, 104 pages, softbound, $14.95

• **Nancy Crow: Quilts and Influences** by Nancy Crow
#1981: AQS, 1990, 256 pages, hardcover, $29.95

• **No Dragons on My Quilt** by Jean Ray Laury with
Ritva Laury and Lizabeth Laury
#2153: AQS, 1990, 52 pages, hardcover, $12.95

• **Oklahoma Heritage Quilts** Oklahoma Quilt Heritage Project
#2032: AQS, 1990, 144 pages, softbound, $19.95

• **Quiltmaker's Guide: Basics & Beyond** by Carol Doak
#2284: AQS, 1992, 208 pages, softbound $19.95

• **QUILTS: The Permanent Collection – MAQS**
#2257: AQS, 1991, 100 pages, 10 x 6½, softbound, $9.95

• **Scarlet Ribbons: American Indian Technique for Today's Quilters**
by Helen Kelley
#1819: AQS, 1987, 104 pages, softbound, $15.95

• **Sets & Borders** by Gwen Marston and Joe Cunningham
#1821: AQS, 1987, 104 pages, softbound, $14.95

• **Somewhere in Between: Quilts and Quilters of Illinois**
by Rita Barrow Barber
#1790: AQS, 1986, 78 pages, softbound, $14.95

• **Stenciled Quilts for Christmas** by Marie Monteith Sturmer
#2098: AQS, 1990, 104 pages, softbound, $14.95

• **Texas Quilts – Texas Treasures** Texas Heritage Quilt Society
#1760: AQS, 1986, 160 pages, hardbound, $24.95

• **A Treasury of Quilting Designs** by Linda Goodmon Emery
#2029: AQS, 1990, 80 pages, 14 x 11, spiral-bound, $14.95

• **Wonderful Wearables: A Celebration of Creative Clothing**
by Virginia Avery
#2286: AQS, 1991, 168 pages, softbound, $24.95

These books can be found in local bookstores and quilt shops. If you are unable to locate a title in your area, you can order by mail from AQS, P.O. Box 3290, Paducah, KY 42002-3290. Please add $1 for the first book and 40¢ for each additional one to cover postage and handling.